How to draw Pokemon

50 Pokemons to Learn to Draw

Copyright © OSIE

Interior designed by OSIE.

Copyright © 2018
OSIE
All rights reserved.
ISBN-13: 978-1986177573
ISBN-10: 1986177572

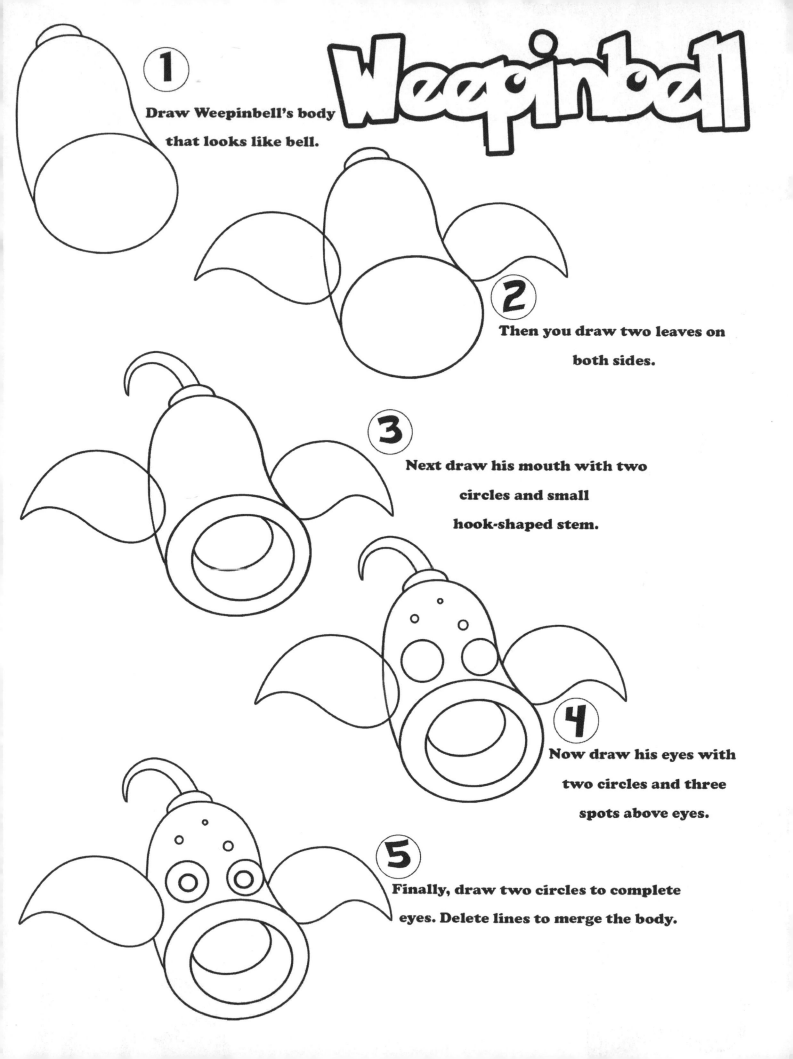

Weepinbell

1 Draw Weepinbell's body that looks like bell.

2 Then you draw two leaves on both sides.

3 Next draw his mouth with two circles and small hook-shaped stem.

4 Now draw his eyes with two circles and three spots above eyes.

5 Finally, draw two circles to complete eyes. Delete lines to merge the body.

Swalot

1 Draw Swalot's body that reminds of ghost's.

2 Then you draw its arms with three fingers.

3 Next draw its eyes and mouth with two big lips.

4 Now draw its long whiskers.

5 Finally, draw rhombs on its body. Delete lines to merge the body.

1

Draw Bewear's head with three-pointed hair and a diamond-shaped muzzle.

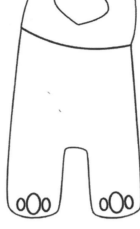

2

Then you draw its body with two legs with pads on the paws.

3

Next draw its hands with a paw on the hand it is waving with.

4

Now draw its band across the top of head with two tufts at each end.

5

Finally, draw eyes and finish nose. Delete lines to merge the body.

Chansey

1 Draw Chansey's ovoid body that resembles an egg.

2 Then you draw a pouch in the middle of its belly contaning an egg in it and a short tail.

3 Next draw its three hair-like growths on the each side of head.

4 Now draw its stubby arms and small feet.

5 Finally, draw its eyes and mouth. Delete lines to merge the body.

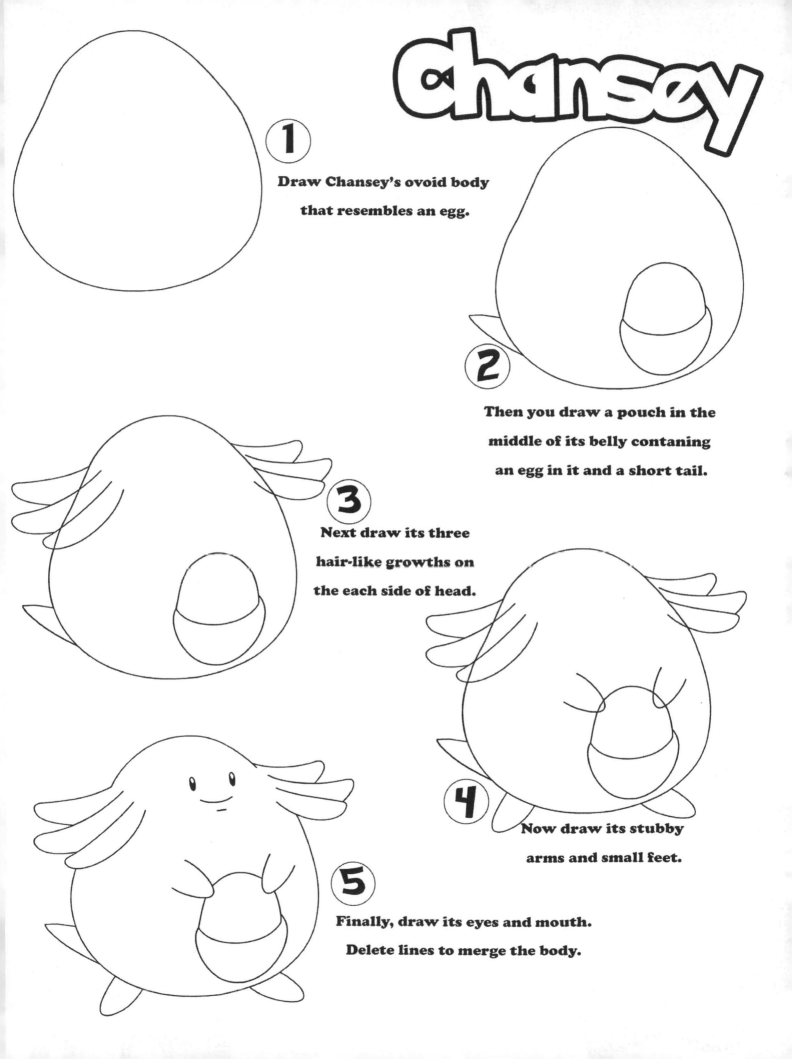

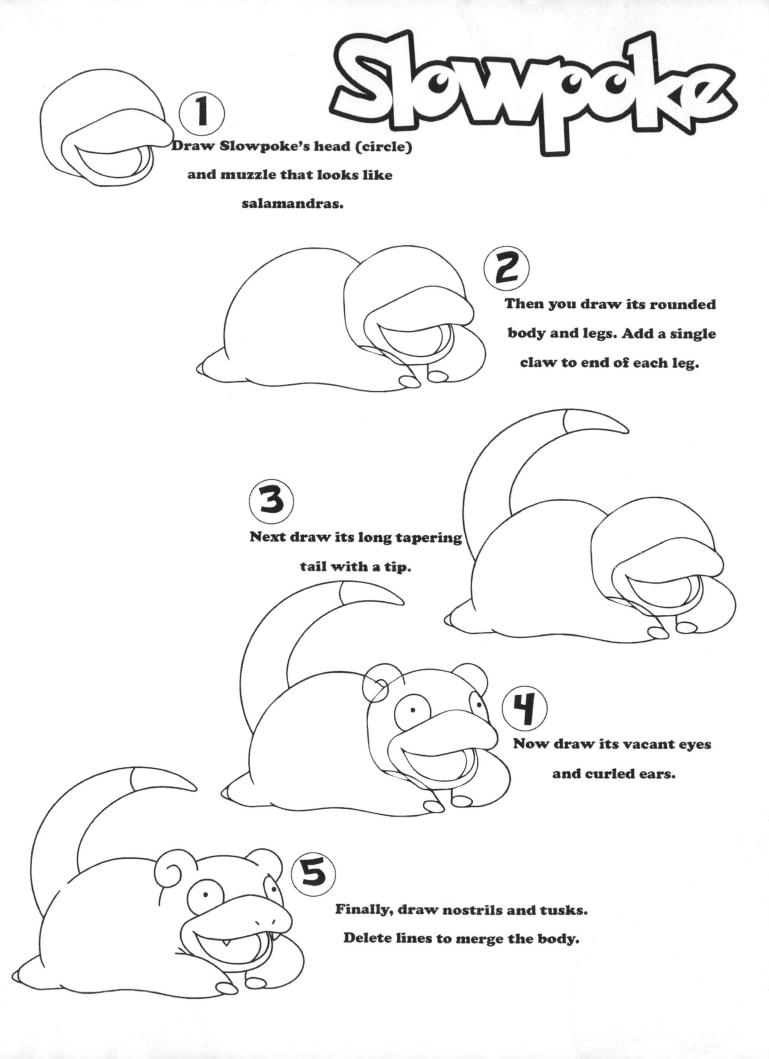

Slowpoke

1 Draw Slowpoke's head (circle) and muzzle that looks like salamandras.

2 Then you draw its rounded body and legs. Add a single claw to end of each leg.

3 Next draw its long tapering tail with a tip.

4 Now draw its vacant eyes and curled ears.

5 Finally, draw nostrils and tusks. Delete lines to merge the body.

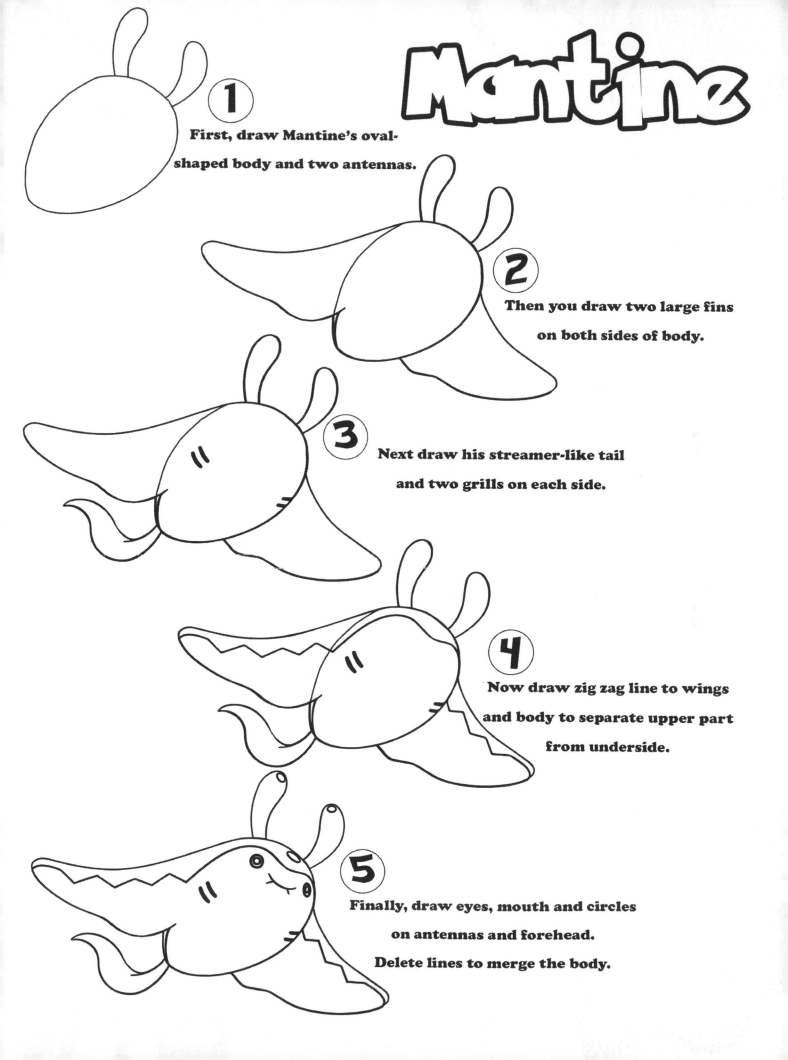

Mantine

1. First, draw Mantine's oval-shaped body and two antennas.

2. Then you draw two large fins on both sides of body.

3. Next draw his streamer-like tail and two grills on each side.

4. Now draw zig zag line to wings and body to separate upper part from underside.

5. Finally, draw eyes, mouth and circles on antennas and forehead. Delete lines to merge the body.

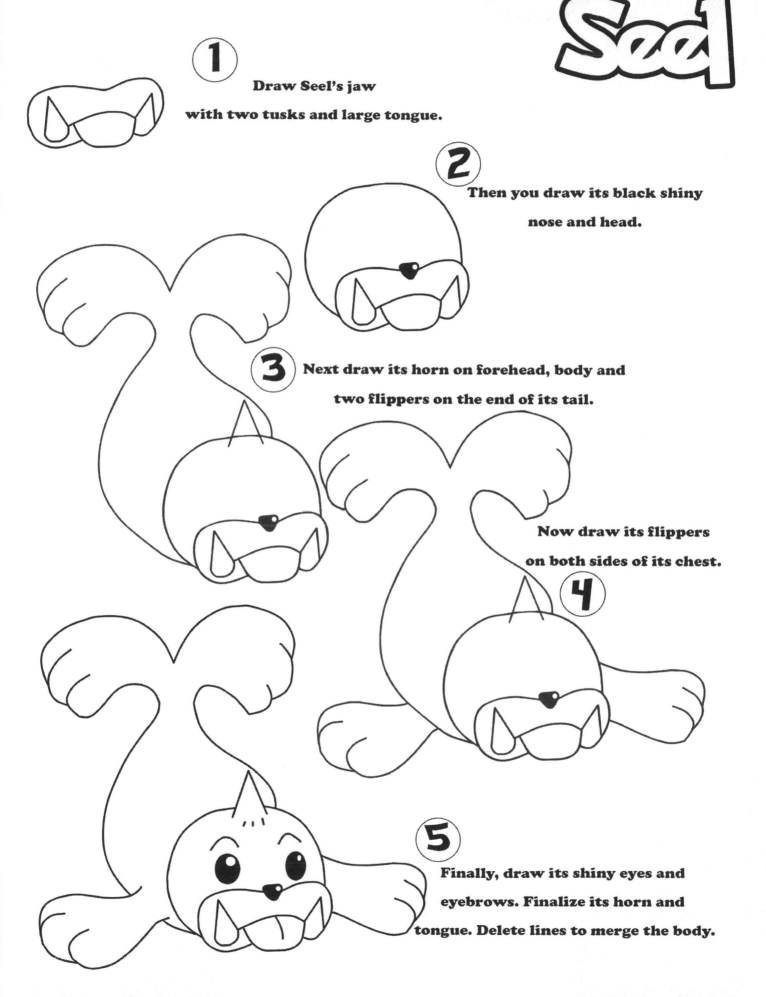

Seel

1 Draw Seel's jaw with two tusks and large tongue.

2 Then you draw its black shiny nose and head.

3 Next draw its horn on forehead, body and two flippers on the end of its tail.

4 Now draw its flippers on both sides of its chest.

5 Finally, draw its shiny eyes and eyebrows. Finalize its horn and tongue. Delete lines to merge the body.

1 First, draw Snorlax's face and tummy that reminds of cloud.

2 Then you draw head with two spiky ears and a big stomach.

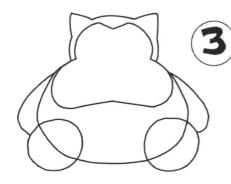

3 Next draw his arms in both sides of stomachand legs as two circles.

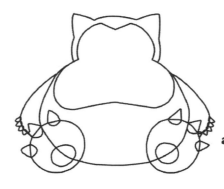

4 Now draw claws to arms, finish legs with large three claws.

5 Finally, draw eyes with two lines and mouth with two fangs. Delete lines to merge the body.

Shroomish

1. Draw Shroomish's top of body that is frilled and looks like top of mushroom.

2. Then you draw the bottom of its body and round feet.

3. Next draw an opening at the top of its body.

4. Now draw two circles on its cheeks and two higher.

5. Finally, draw its eyes, line for forehead and mouth. Delete lines to merge the body.

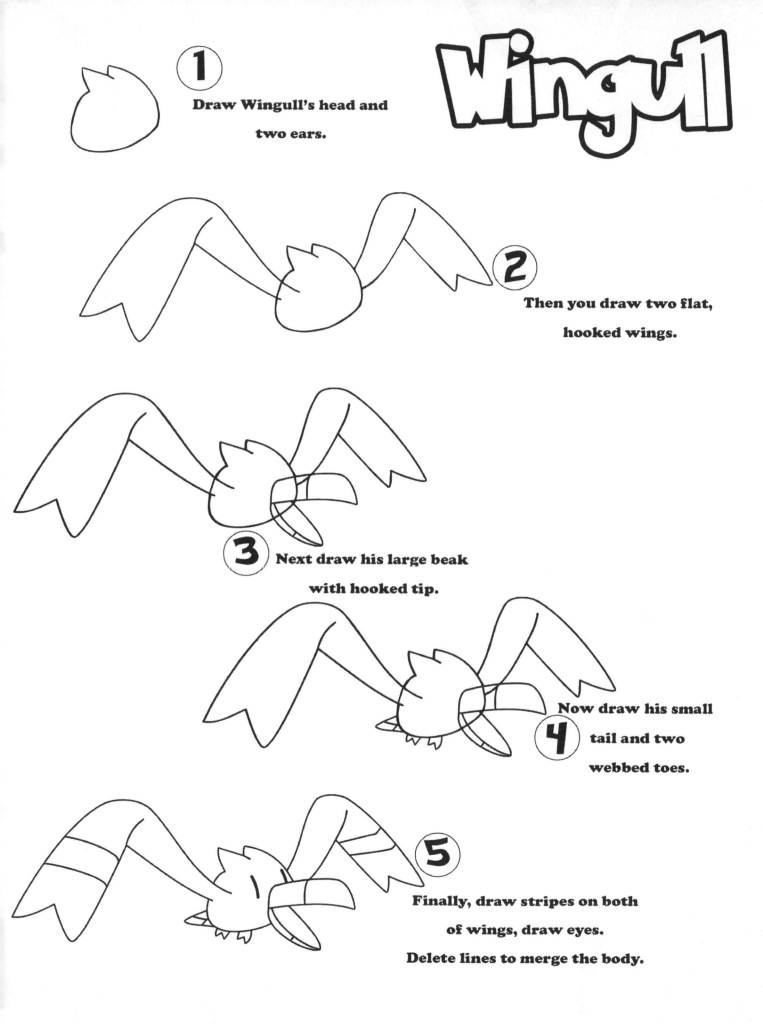

1 Draw Wingull's head and two ears.

Wingull

2 Then you draw two flat, hooked wings.

3 Next draw his large beak with hooked tip.

4 Now draw his small tail and two webbed toes.

5 Finally, draw stripes on both of wings, draw eyes. Delete lines to merge the body.

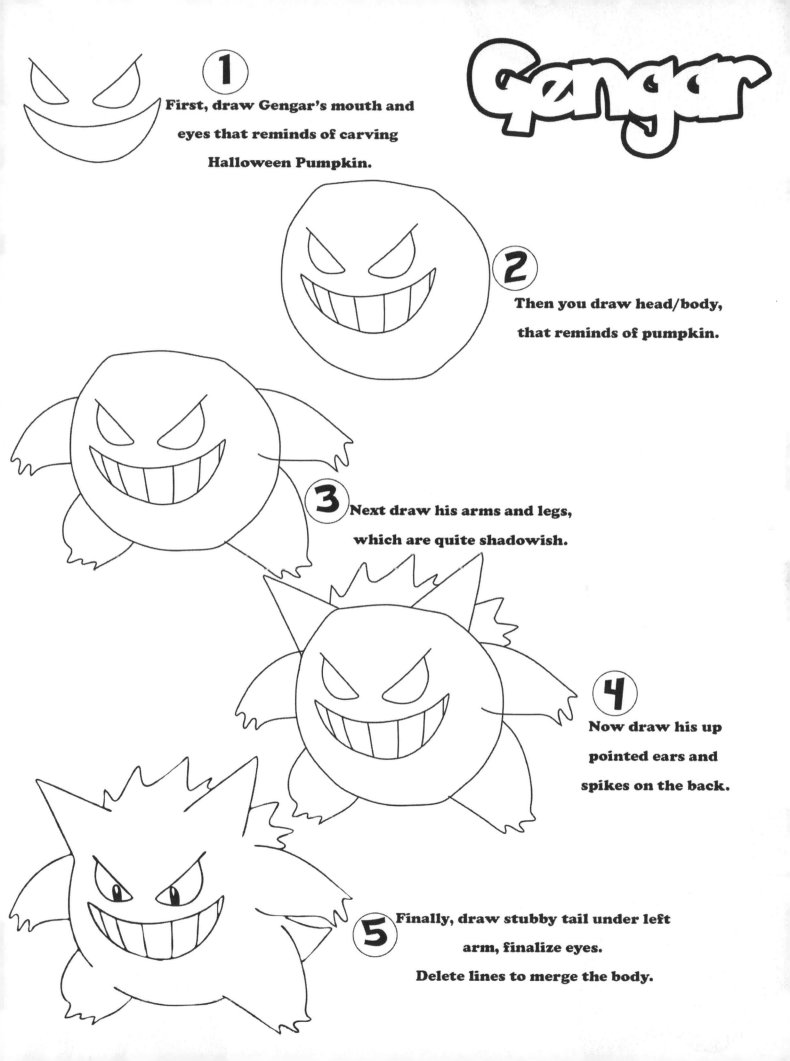

1 First, draw Gengar's mouth and eyes that reminds of carving Halloween Pumpkin.

Gengar

2 Then you draw head/body, that reminds of pumpkin.

3 Next draw his arms and legs, which are quite shadowish.

4 Now draw his up pointed ears and spikes on the back.

5 Finally, draw stubby tail under left arm, finalize eyes. Delete lines to merge the body.

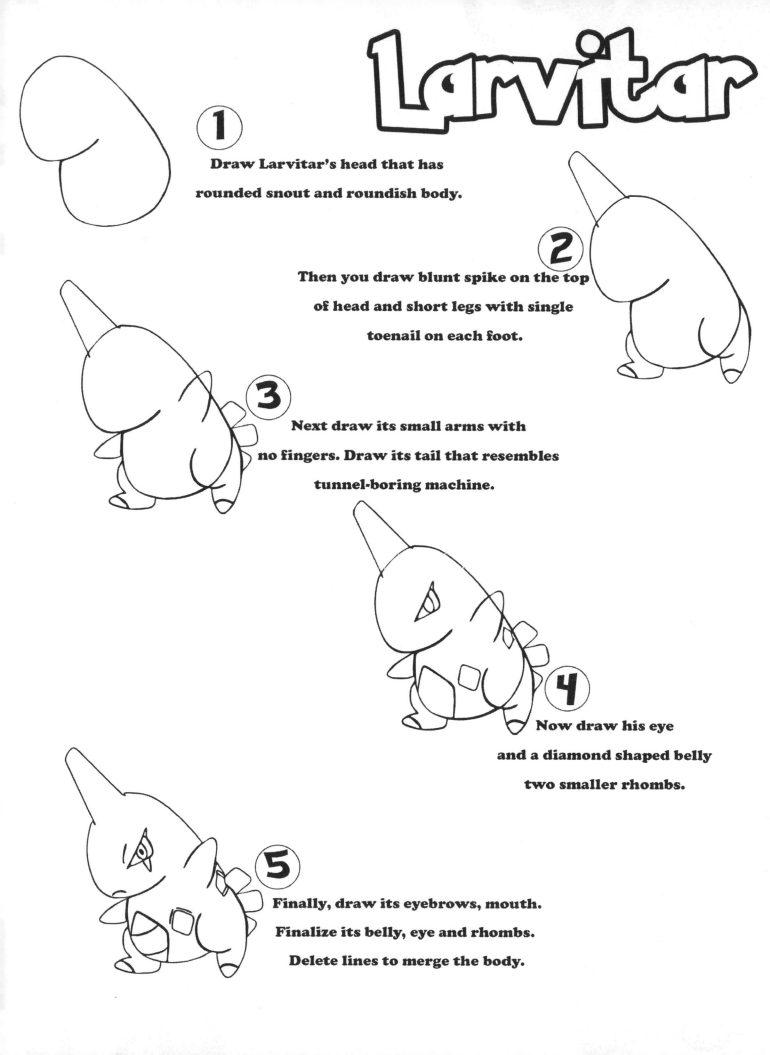

Larvitar

1

Draw Larvitar's head that has rounded snout and roundish body.

2

Then you draw blunt spike on the top of head and short legs with single toenail on each foot.

3

Next draw its small arms with no fingers. Draw its tail that resembles tunnel-boring machine.

4

Now draw his eye and a diamond shaped belly two smaller rhombs.

5

Finally, draw its eyebrows, mouth. Finalize its belly, eye and rhombs. Delete lines to merge the body.

1

Draw Bibarel's short snout, mouth and protruding upper incisors.

2

Then you draw its eyes, face with extenison over each eye and its head that looks like a cloud.

3

Next draw its body and feet that have three toes.

4

Now draw his short arms, circle on chest and flat tail.

5

Finally, draw two circles on feet, two wavy lines on its tail and a small nose. Finalize eyes, legs. Delete lines to merge the body.

Charmander

1

Draw Charmander's head and body that reminds bit of bowling pin. Add nose and jaw to the left side.

2

Then draw arms with 3 claws and legs.

3

Next draw his tail and eyes. To draw his tummy continue line from left leg up, and to draw mouth start from nose.

4

Now draw claws on legs, fire on the top of tail. Add two eyes.

5

Finally, draw the teeth, tongue and nostrils finalize face, right hand and tail. Delete lines to merge the body.

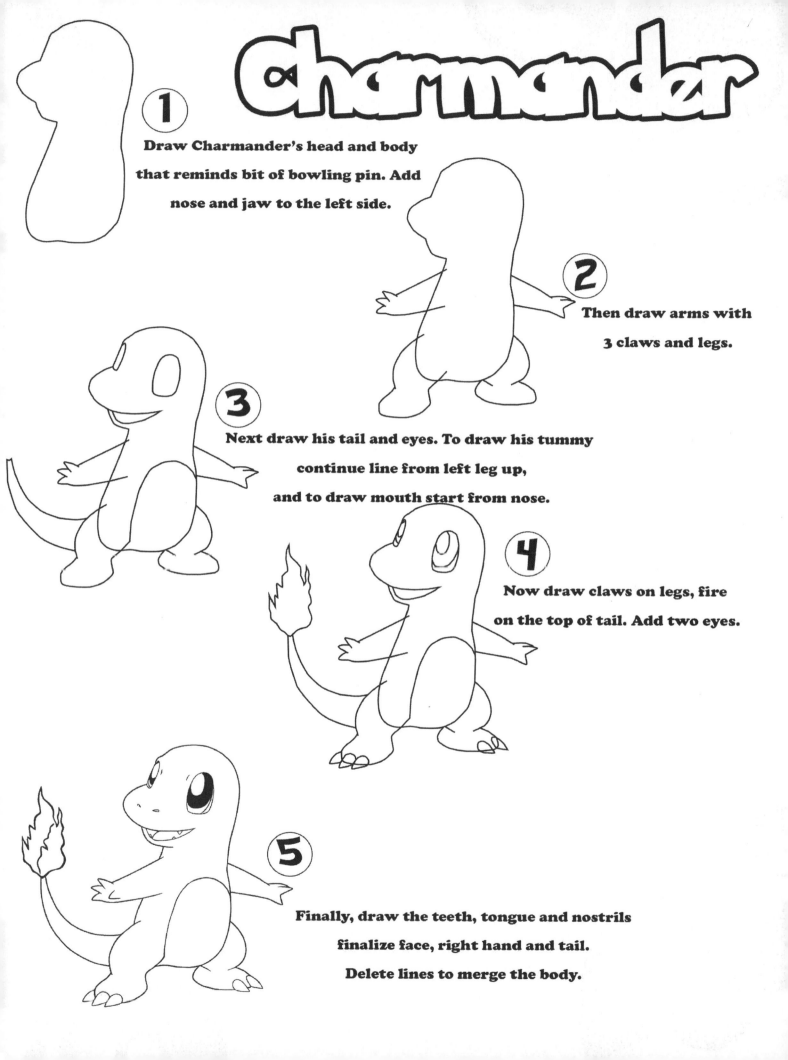

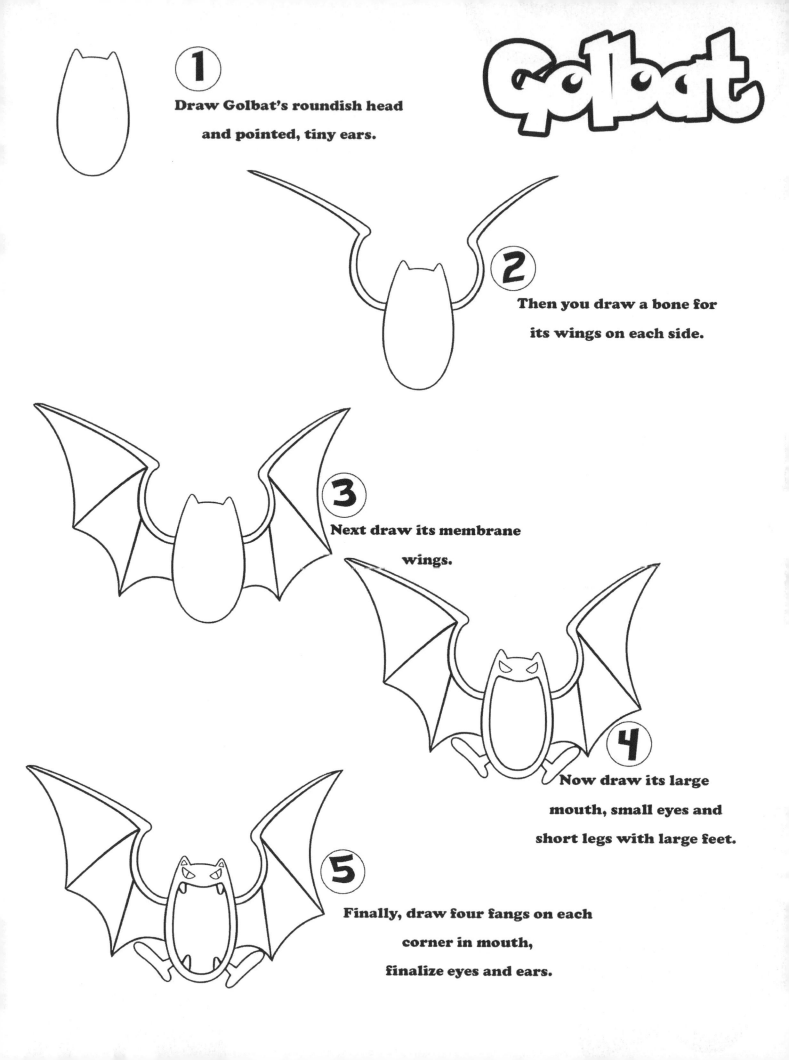

1

Draw Golbat's roundish head
and pointed, tiny ears.

Golbat

2

Then you draw a bone for
its wings on each side.

3

Next draw its membrane
wings.

4

Now draw its large
mouth, small eyes and
short legs with large feet.

5

Finally, draw four fangs on each
corner in mouth,
finalize eyes and ears.

Pikachu

1 Draw Pikachu's head (circle) and body that looks like rouded bell shape.

2 Then you draw two ears similar to rabbit's, draw arms and feet.

3 Next draw its tail behind his left arm with two parallel zig zag lines.

4 Now draw its eyes with two circles and mouth.

5 Finally, draw two circles on cheeks, finalize ears, arms and legs. Delete lines to merge the body.

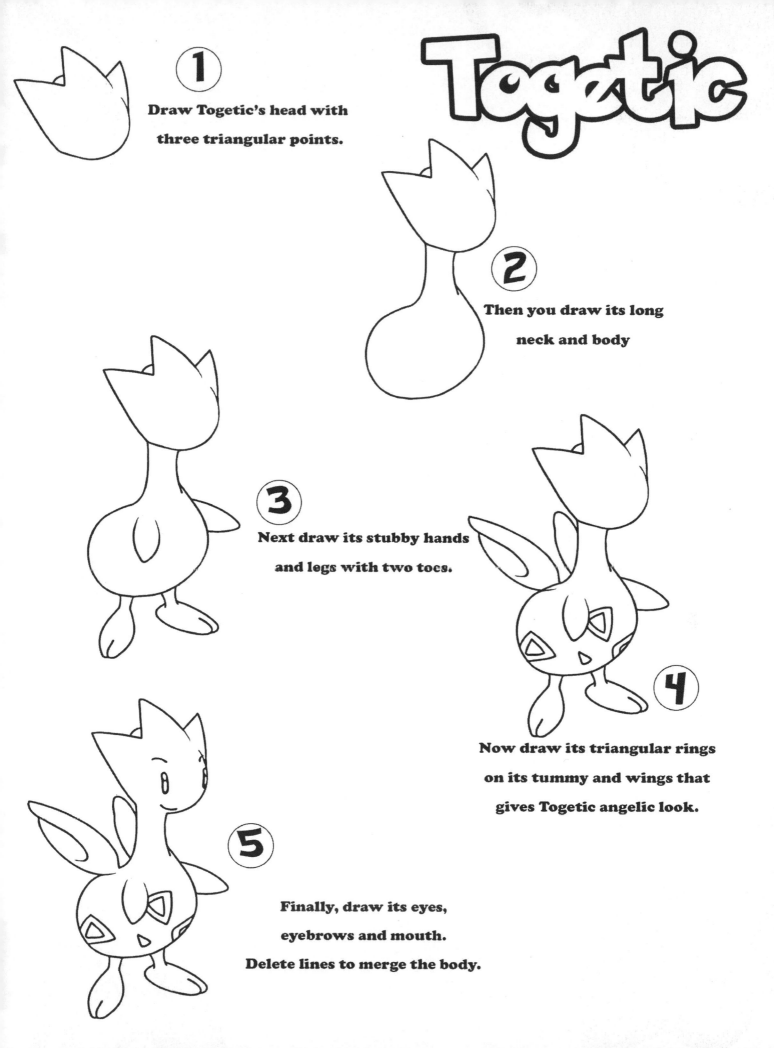

1 Draw Togetic's head with three triangular points.

Togetic

2 Then you draw its long neck and body

3 Next draw its stubby hands and legs with two toes.

4 Now draw its triangular rings on its tummy and wings that gives Togetic angelic look.

5 Finally, draw its eyes, eyebrows and mouth. Delete lines to merge the body.

Bulbasaur

1 Draw Bulbasaur's head as flatted circle and eyes that looks like cave opening and a regural mouth.

2 Then draw the bulb that reminds of garlic's bulb behind the head.

3 Next draw his legs and body under the bulb and head, then add ears.

4 Now draw markings on head and legs. Add to eyes and draw a zig zag top on bulb as a crown.

5 Finally, draw the claws, finalize face, eyes and mouth. Delete lines to merge the body.

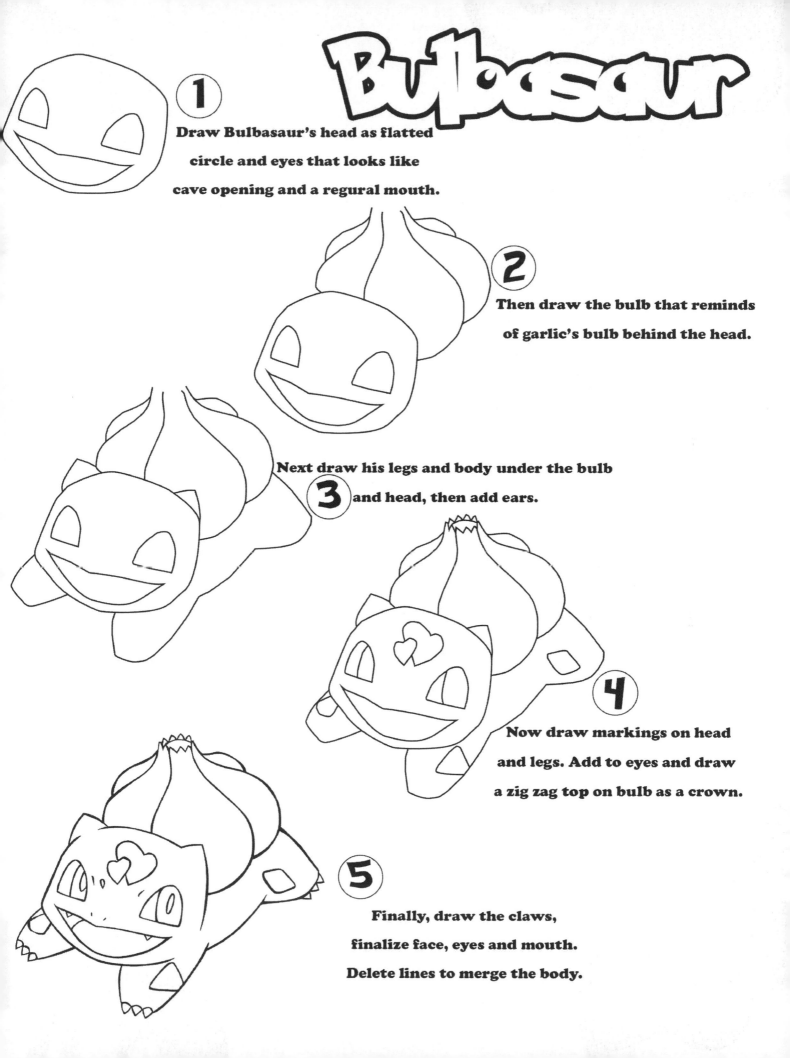

Jirachi

1 Draw Jirachi's head that has three points extended.

2 Then you draw its body and short legs and arms with flaps on the underside that look like long sleeves.

3 Form its face by drawing extensions on both sides. On each of three points draw a tag, known as a "wish tag".

4 Now draw its eyes with two circles on face and one on its tummy. Draw two streamers flowing from its back.

5 Finally, draw its mouth and finalize eyes. Delete lines to merge the body.

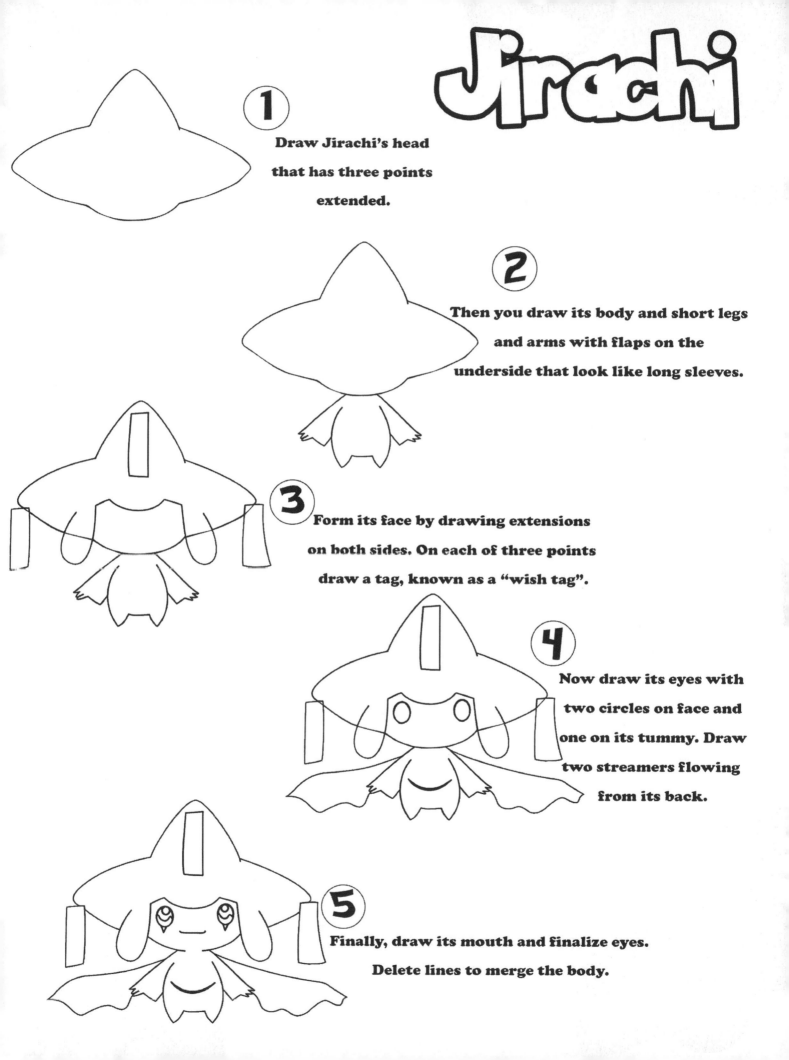

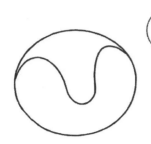

1 Draw Piplup's head (circle) and nose and forehead.

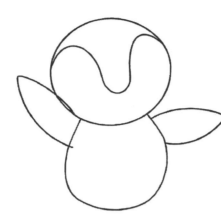

2 Then you draw its body and two flipper-like arms with no fingers.

3 Next draw its cape-like feathers around the neck, two ovals on the chest and crown like line on the forehead.

4 Now draw its small feet with three toes, tail and eyes.

5 Finally, draw a short beak, finalize eyes. Delete lines to merge the body.

1

Draw Quilladin's three-pointed patch, head and triangles that mark its cheeks.

2

Then you draw armor-like shell with three-pointed patch on tummy and two large spines as its ears.

3

Next draw lower part of its body, legs with two toes and tail behind.

4

Now draw its clawed arms, nose, eyes and eyebrows.

5

Finally, draw mouth, finalize ears, arms and eyes. Delete lines to merge the body.

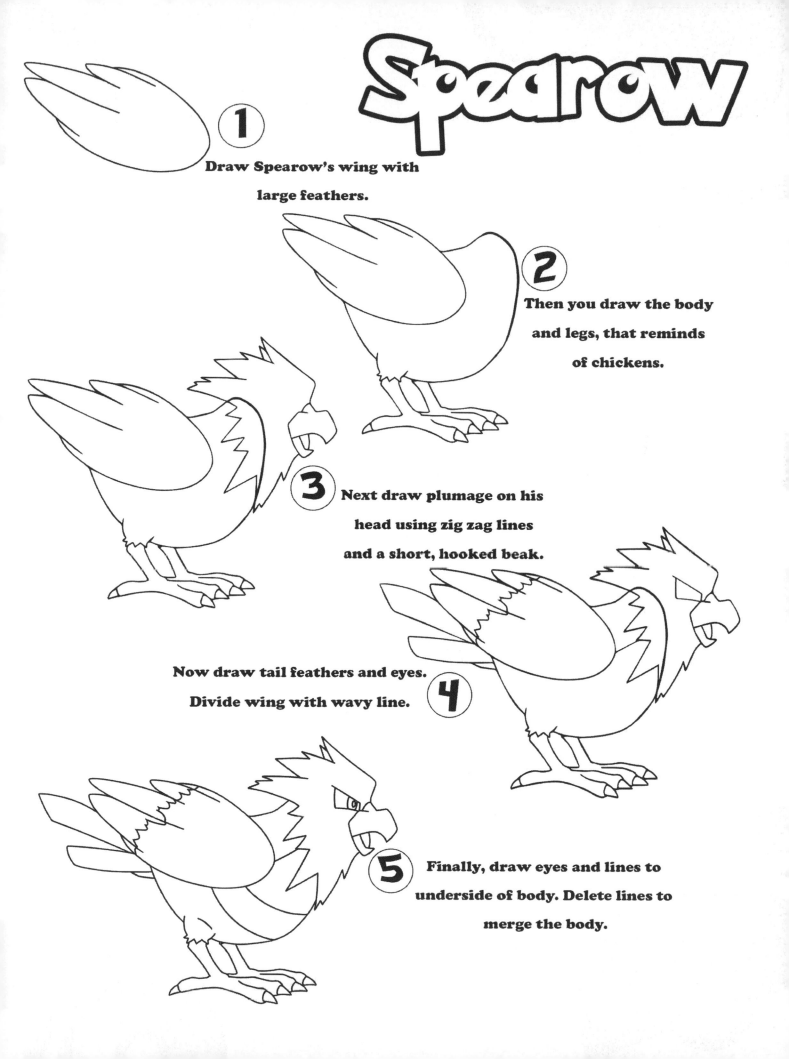

Spearow

1 Draw Spearow's wing with large feathers.

2 Then you draw the body and legs, that reminds of chickens.

3 Next draw plumage on his head using zig zag lines and a short, hooked beak.

Now draw tail feathers and eyes. Divide wing with wavy line. **4**

5 Finally, draw eyes and lines to underside of body. Delete lines to merge the body.

1

Draw Buizel's head
that reminds of weasel's.

2

Then you draw collar around
its neck, long body and
tummy.

3

Next draw its arms and legs,
each with 3 fingers.
Draw fins on underside of arms.

4

Now draw its tail that splits
in two tips and draw spots on top
of eyes.

5

Finally, draw eyes, nose and mouth.
Draw two parallel marks on its cheeks.
Delete lines to merge the body.

Marowak

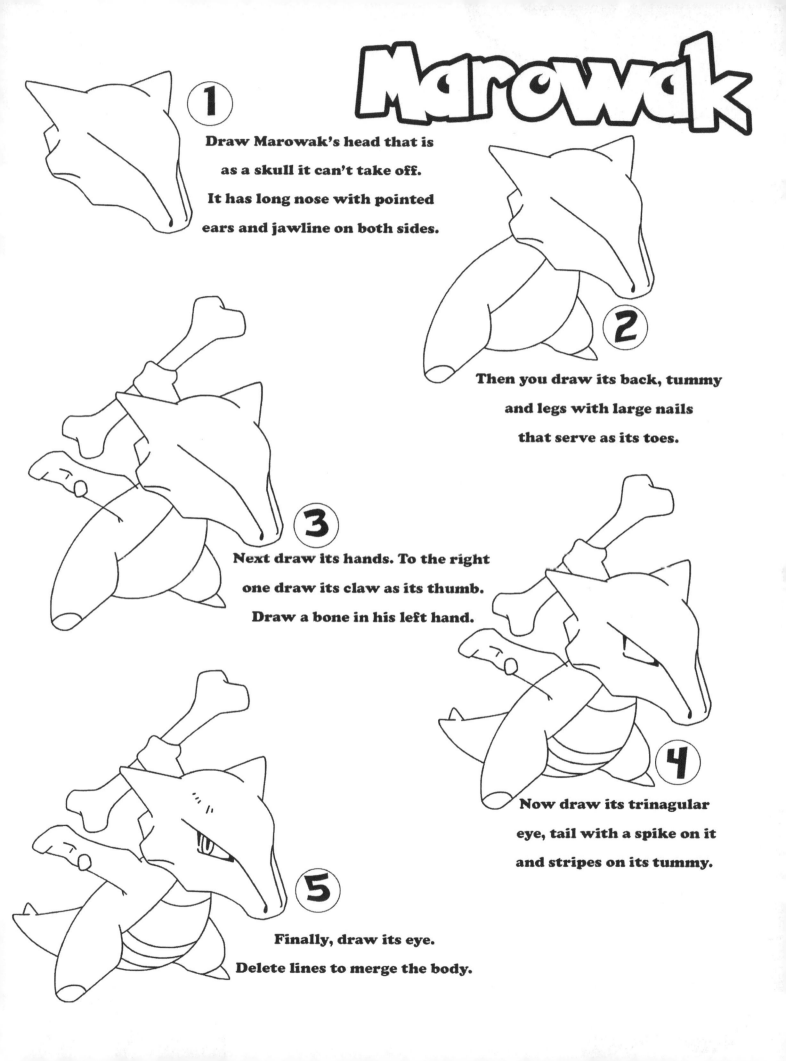

1 Draw Marowak's head that is as a skull it can't take off. It has long nose with pointed ears and jawline on both sides.

2 Then you draw its back, tummy and legs with large nails that serve as its toes.

3 Next draw its hands. To the right one draw its claw as its thumb. Draw a bone in his left hand.

4 Now draw its trinagular eye, tail with a spike on it and stripes on its tummy.

5 Finally, draw its eye. Delete lines to merge the body.

1
Draw Oddish's flat head (oval).

2
Then you draw two oval feet.

3
Next draw his five large leaves that sprout from his head.

4
Now draw his eyes with two circles and mouth.

5
Finally, finalize leaves. Delete lines to merge the body.

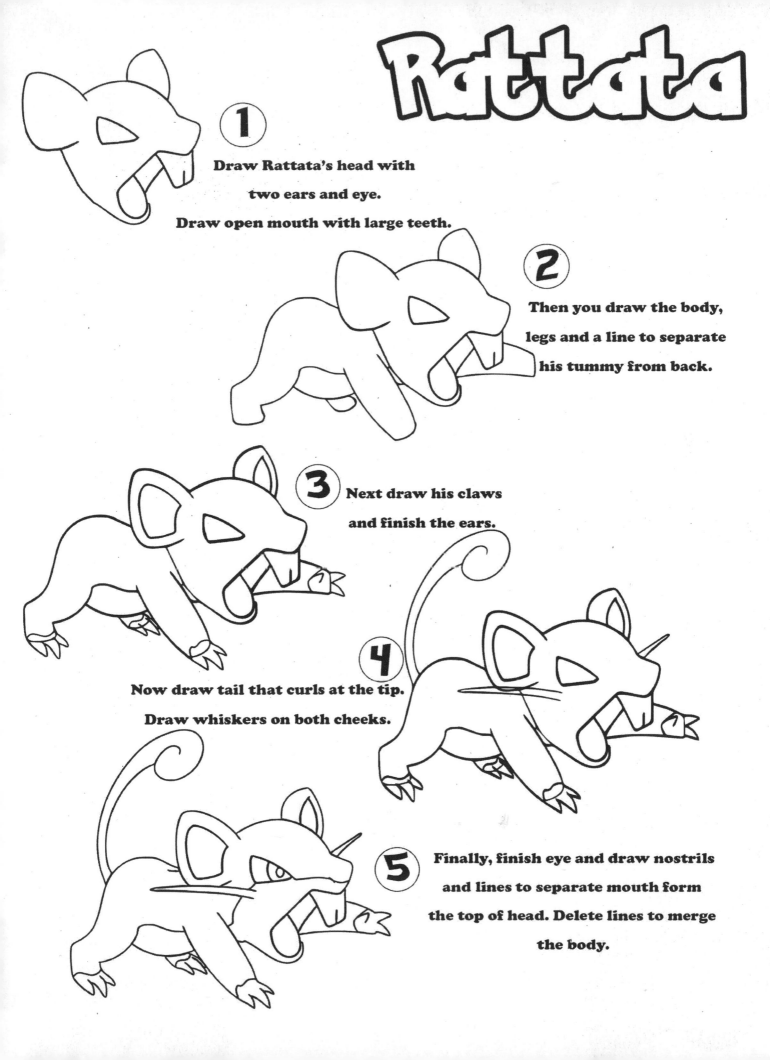

Rattata

1 Draw Rattata's head with two ears and eye. Draw open mouth with large teeth.

2 Then you draw the body, legs and a line to separate his tummy from back.

3 Next draw his claws and finish the ears.

Now draw tail that curls at the tip. Draw whiskers on both cheeks.

4

5 Finally, finish eye and draw nostrils and lines to separate mouth form the top of head. Delete lines to merge the body.

1

Draw Hypno's head with triangular ears and large nose.

2

Then you draw its white fur ruff by drawing zig zag line around its neck.

3

Next draw its hands that are similar to humans.

4

Now draw its body, legs with three toes on each foot and a pendulum in his hand used for hypnosis.

5

Finally, draw its eyes, finalize ears, pendulum and body. Delete lines to merge the body.

Marshtomp

1 Draw Marshtomp's head that looks like a football and body wtih two legs.

2 Then you draw two fins to each side of body.

3 Next draw his wings behind his back and angular fin on the top of the head.

4 Now draw his eyes, belly, gills on the ends of both cheeks and a big mouth.

5 Finally, draw nostrils, finalize eyes, mouth and legs. Delete lines to merge the body.

1

Draw Tauros's rounded muzzle, eyes and then horns on each side at the top of head.

2

Then you draw the fur mane behind his head.

3 Next draw his body and legs. Add a hoof at the end of each leg.

4 Now draw his three tails with a tuft of fur at each end.

5 Finally, draw three bumps on his forehead, mouth and nostrils. Finalize horns.

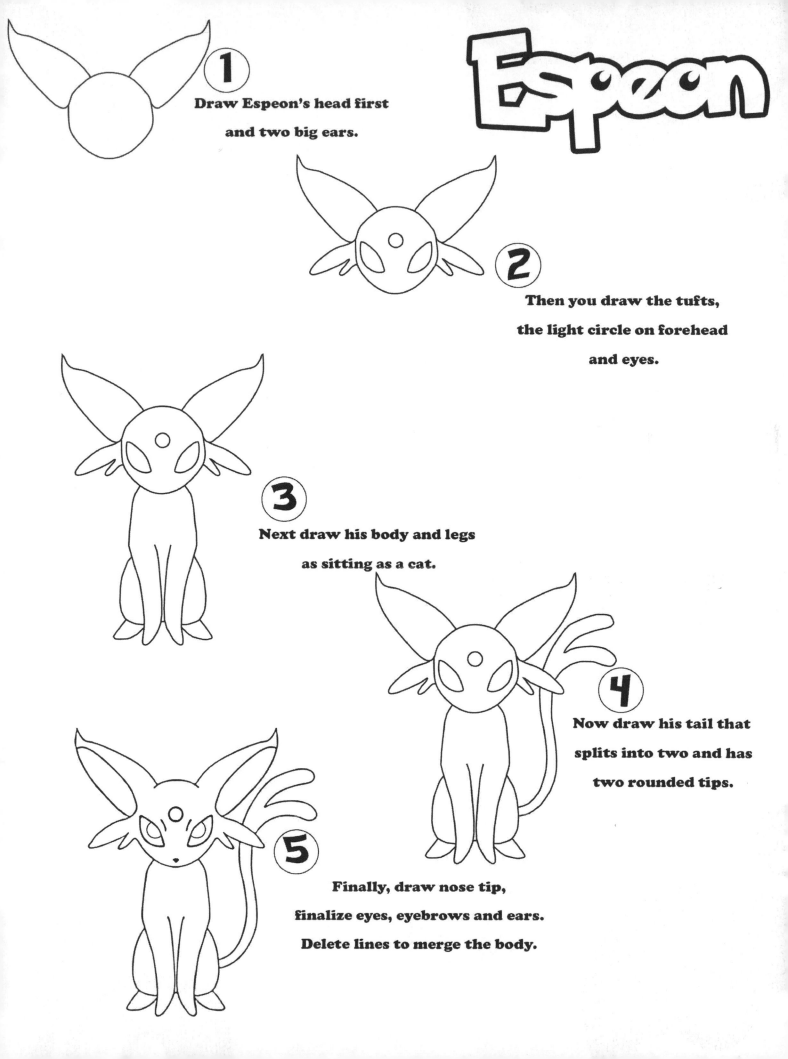

1 Draw Espeon's head first and two big ears.

Espeon

2 Then you draw the tufts, the light circle on forehead and eyes.

3 Next draw his body and legs as sitting as a cat.

4 Now draw his tail that splits into two and has two rounded tips.

5 Finally, draw nose tip, finalize eyes, eyebrows and ears. Delete lines to merge the body.

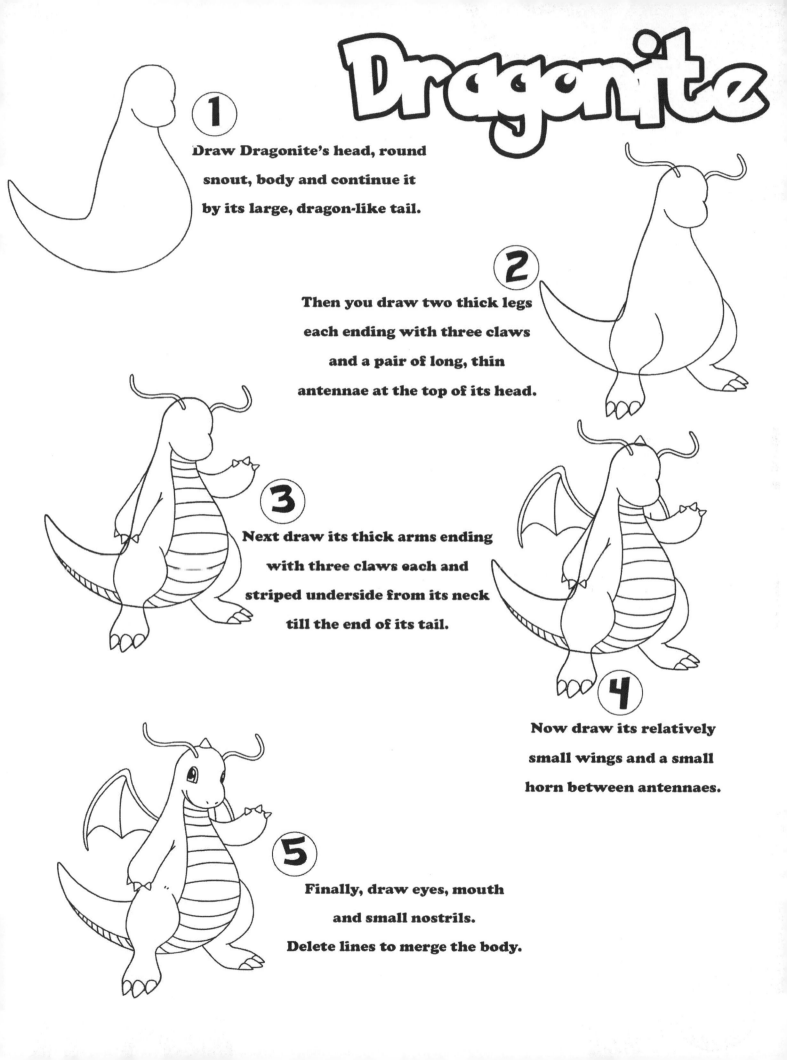

Dragonite

1 Draw Dragonite's head, round snout, body and continue it by its large, dragon-like tail.

2 Then you draw two thick legs each ending with three claws and a pair of long, thin antennae at the top of its head.

3 Next draw its thick arms ending with three claws each and striped underside from its neck till the end of its tail.

4 Now draw its relatively small wings and a small horn between antennaes.

5 Finally, draw eyes, mouth and small nostrils. Delete lines to merge the body.

1

Draw Eevee's head
and fur on the forehead
that looks like head of
a small boy.

2

Then you draw its large furry
collar around the neck.

3

Next draw its body and four
short legs each with three toes.
Draw Eevee's eyes and mouh.

4

Now draw bushy tail
and long pointed
ears.

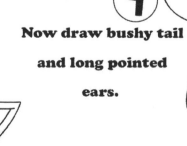

5

Finally, draw a nose, eyebrows and
zig zag line to tail, finalize eyes.
Delete lines to merge the body.

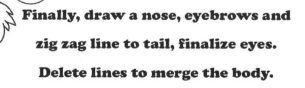

1 Draw Machop's hair first that looks like 3 axe heads.

2 Then you draw head, mouth and eyes.

3 Next draw his arms and fists. Add fingers to fists.

4 Now draw his body, legs and tail, which is behind the back.

5 Finally, add six lines to chest and ribs, finalize legs, face and eyes. Delete lines to merge the body.

Parasect

1 Draw Parasect's mushroom under which most of its body is.

2 Then you draw its two large pincers on each side and two circles in middle as its eyes.

3 Next draw its head, body and two rear legs on each side.

4 Now draw circles on mushroom to make it look parasitic.

5 Finally, draw mouth, finalize mushroom, pincers. Delete lines to merge the body.

Meowth

1 Draw Meowth's head with two ears and gold oval coin embedded in its forehead.

2 Then you draw two whiskers on each cheek and two near ears ponting upwards. Draw eyes and mouth.

3 Next draw its tummy and two paws pointing up behind the head.

4 Now draw its curled tail pointed upwards and its legs and huge feet.

5 Finally, draw two small teeth, finalize eyes. Delete lines to merge the body.

1 Draw Froakie's head that reminds of football and oval eyes on the top.

2 Then you draw cloudy ruffle around face and neck and draw nose.

3 Next draw his body and legs as sitting as a frog like pose.

4 Now draw his eyes with two oval circles and both hands.

5 Finally, draw mouth, finalize eyes, arms and feet. Delete lines to merge the body.

Mamoswine

1 Draw Mamoswine's muzzle, snook and mask-like pattern that resembles ski goggles.

2 Then you draw the outside of pattern and its round body.

3 Next draw its four fury legs each with three thick toes.

4 Now draw its tusks.

5 Finally, draw its black, deep eyes, and nostrils.
Delete lines to merge the body.

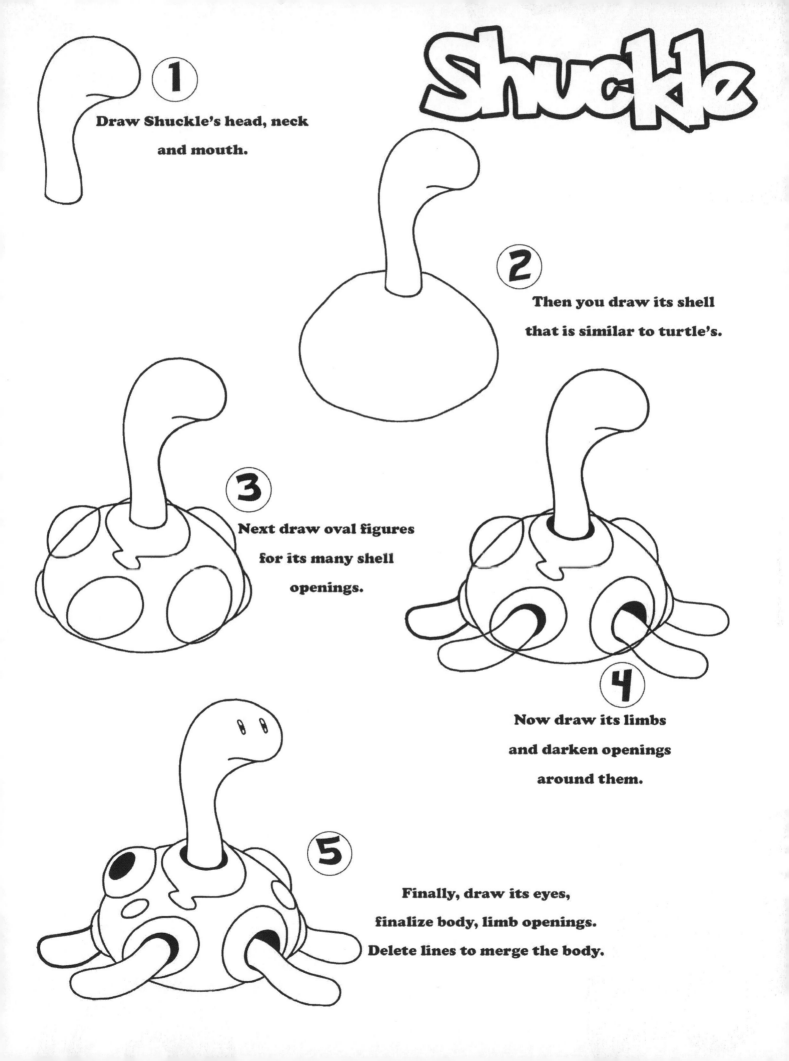

Shuckle

1 Draw Shuckle's head, neck and mouth.

2 Then you draw its shell that is similar to turtle's.

3 Next draw oval figures for its many shell openings.

4 Now draw its limbs and darken openings around them.

5 Finally, draw its eyes, finalize body, limb openings. Delete lines to merge the body.

Tentacool

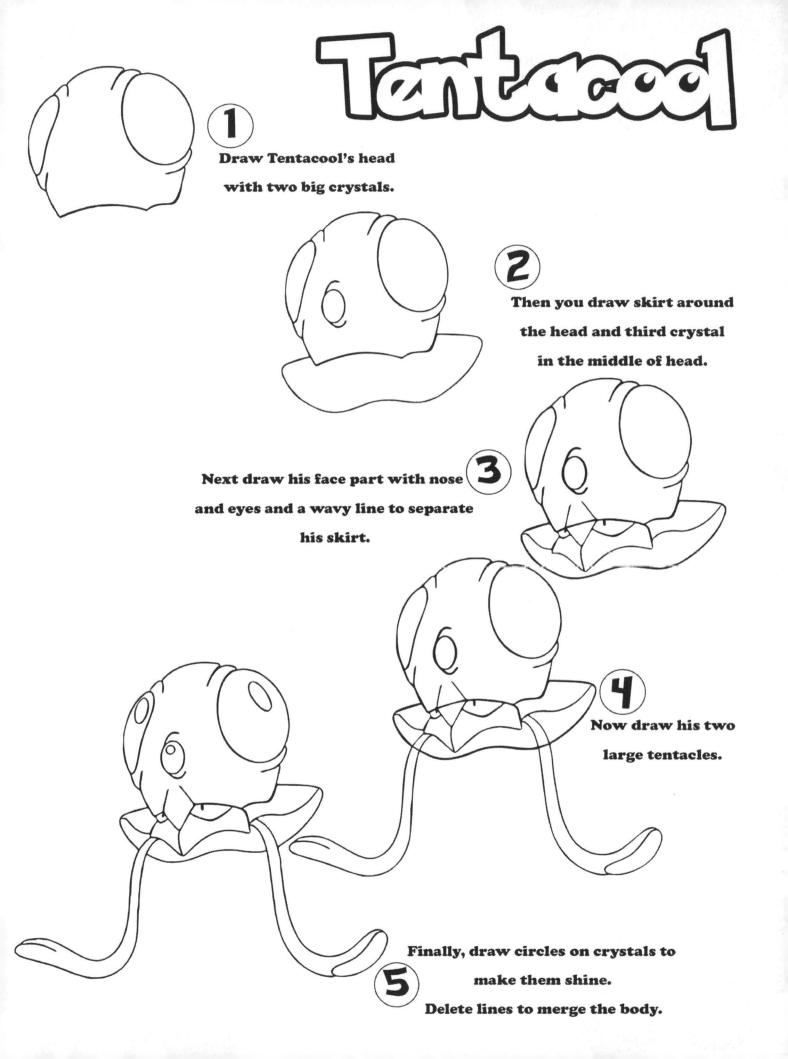

1 Draw Tentacool's head with two big crystals.

2 Then you draw skirt around the head and third crystal in the middle of head.

Next draw his face part with nose **3** and eyes and a wavy line to separate his skirt.

4 Now draw his two large tentacles.

Finally, draw circles on crystals to make them shine. **5** Delete lines to merge the body.

(1)

Draw Pyroar's face
that reminds of iron man mask.

(2)

Then you draw front of its
dominant fur mane that resembles
the Daimonji 大 symbol.

(3)

Next draw rear part of its mane
and front legs each with three toes.

(4)

Now draw its body,
rear fury legs and
long, noble tail.

(5)

Finally, draw mouth, eyes and
a zig zag line to its front legs.
Finalize nose and paws.

1 Draw Lugia's long neck and head.

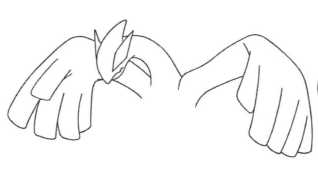

2 Then you draw two huge wings that look like big hands.

3 Next draw his body and legs, which reminds of kangaroo's legs with three fingers.

4 Now draw his tail and protrusions on his back and two pointed ones at the end of his tail.

5 Finally, draw eyes finalize body.

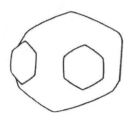

1

Draw Sableye's head that is in form of hexagon, as well as two big eyes in the same form.

2

Then you draw two long arms with three sharp claws.

3

Next draw its body, legs, a big smile and a line on his forehead.

4

Now draw its big ears and a zig zag line to draw its sharp teeth.

5

Finally, draw eyes as jewels and a jewel on its chest. Delete lines to merge the body.

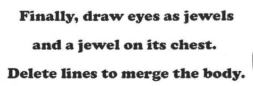

Draw Hitmontop's head with flat,
curved extensions on either side.

Then you draw spike on the top

of head and its tummy.

Next draw its small legs with

large feet with three claws.

Draw a skinny tail that ends with

sphere with a spike on it.

Now draw his arms

that ends with spherical

hands with no digits.

Finally, draw its eyes, mouth.

Finalize feet.

Delete lines to merge the body.

1 Draw Lombre's head with jawline, ears and hair.

Lombre

2 Then you draw its body and two legs with toes as it sits.

3 Next draw its two arms with fingers and his vest.

4 Now draw big mouth and its lilypad that resembles a sombrero.

5 Finally, draw eyes. Delete lines to merge the body.

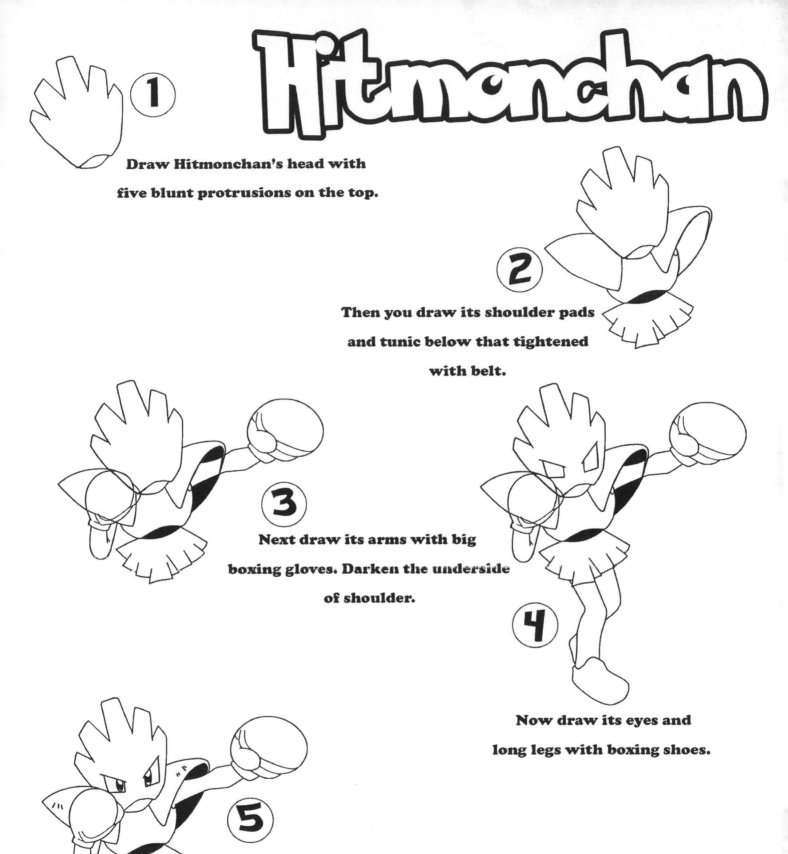

Hitmonchan

1 Draw Hitmonchan's head with five blunt protrusions on the top.

2 Then you draw its shoulder pads and tunic below that tightened with belt.

3 Next draw its arms with big boxing gloves. Darken the underside of shoulder.

4 Now draw its eyes and long legs with boxing shoes.

5 Finalize eyes, shoulders. Delete lines to merge the body.

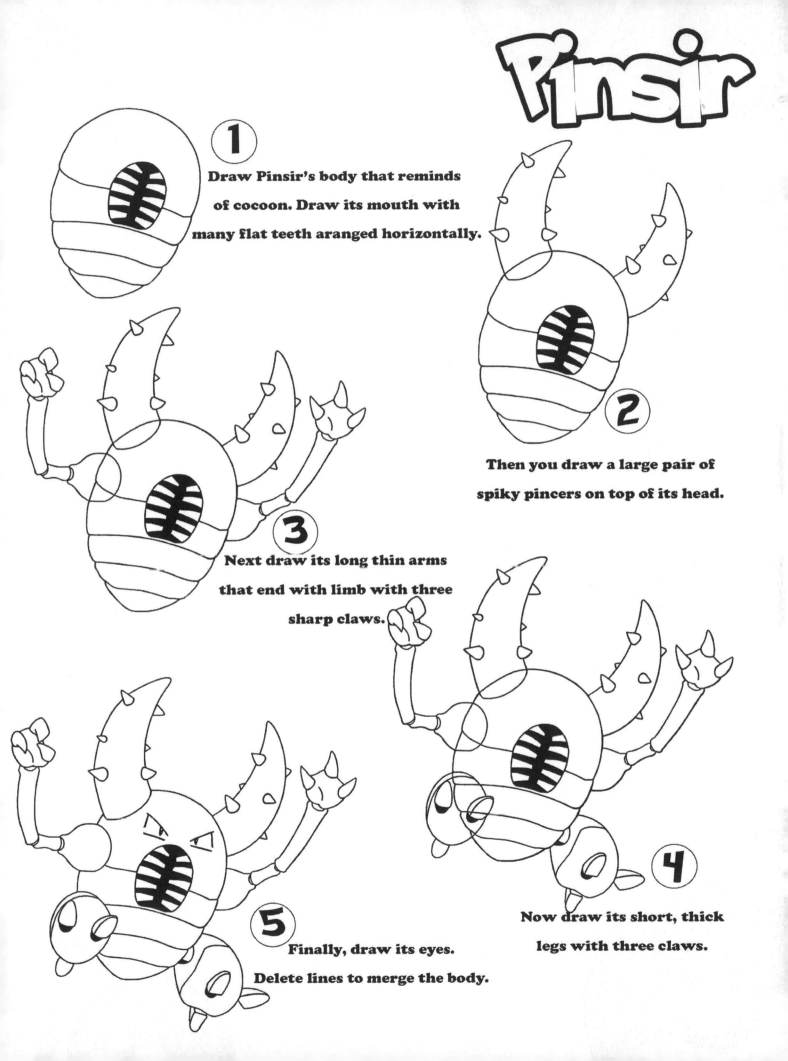

Pinsir

1 Draw Pinsir's body that reminds of cocoon. Draw its mouth with many flat teeth aranged horizontally.

2 Then you draw a large pair of spiky pincers on top of its head.

3 Next draw its long thin arms that end with limb with three sharp claws.

4 Now draw its short, thick legs with three claws.

5 Finally, draw its eyes. Delete lines to merge the body.

Exeggutor

1 Draw Exeggutor's head and body that looks like rouded bell shape.

2 Then you draw legs with two toes and a pad on each foot.

3 Next draw its three heads that remind coconuts.

4 Now draw its eyes, mouths and fangs.

5 Finally, draw two lines on its tummy and one on each leg. Delete lines to merge the body.

Growlithe

1 Draw Growlithe's muzzle with nose and mouth that reminds of dog's. Underneath draw fur on its chest.

2 Then starting from muzzle draw its head, body and legs. Hind paws have three toes each and front paws have two claws each.

3 Next draw its large, round ear, tuft on the top of head and fury tail.

4 Now draw stripes along its back and on legs. Draw eye.

5 Finally, complete eye and delete lines to merge the body.

Sandslash

1 Draw Sandslash's head with narrow muzzle and eyes with nose. Draw the body as well.

2 Then you draw his paws and legs.

3 Next draw sharp quills on the back of his head and back.

4 Now draw two large claws on both legs and paws.

5 Finally, delete lines to merge the body.

1

Draw Luxray's forehead and nose. Then draw big oval ears and a blunt muzzle.

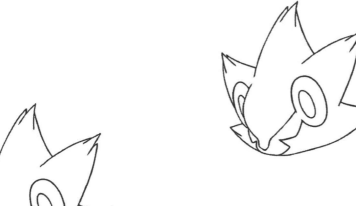

2

Then you draw its head that has a large fur mane on it.

3

Next draw its torso and front hind legs, with large paws.

4

Now draw its body, rear legs and tail, with fury start and the tip with four-pointed star.

5

Finally, draw eyes, nose and mouth. Finalize its front and rear legs. Delete lines to merge the body.

Printed in Great Britain
by Amazon